Sonam The Star

Brian Gueyser

Illustrated by Rick Wenning

Kids At Heart Publishing LLC
PO Box 492
Milton, IN 47357
765-478-5773
www.kidsatheartpublishing.com

Published by Kids At Heart Publishing LLC July 29, 2019.

ISBN 978-1-946171-41-2
Library of Congress Control Number: 2019911051

Published in Milton, Indiana.

This book is printed on acid-free paper.

To order more copies of this book go to
www.kidsatheartpublishing.com.

Kids At Heart Publishing LLC books feature "Turn the Page Technology."
No batteries or charging required.

Dedication

सोनम र मेरो དགོན་པ (गोम्पा)को साथीहरुको लागि

ཕུབས་རྗེ་ཚེ

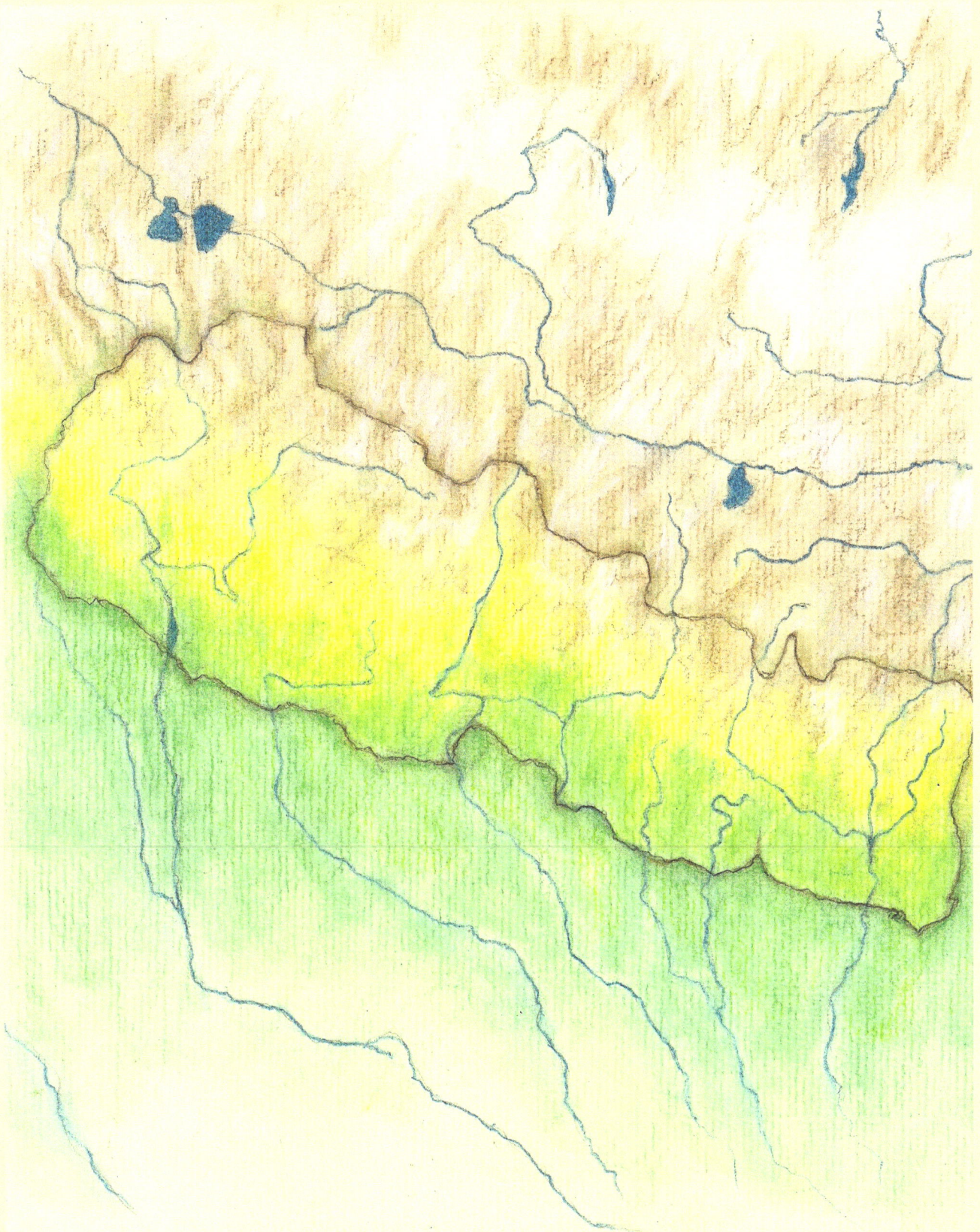

Many years ago I lived in Nepal.

There were many
amazing things I saw there.

There were many
amazing people I met.

And many amazing
foods I ate.

But the most amazing thing of all
was my friend Sonam The Star.

Sonam was a monk at the monastery
where I lived and taught.

Sonam was a happy little monk,
and he was always smiling.

He smiled when he went to morning prayers.

He smiled during school.

He smiled during lunch.

He smiled when he was playing.

I'm sure he even smiled in his sleep. He was always so happy.

But one day, when I saw Sonam
he wasn't smiling. He was looking at the sky.

"Sonam, what do you see?" I asked him.
"My family," he told me softly. Then he
took me by the hand and asked me to sit
beside him.

14

"Sometimes..." he said very quietly now, almost as if he were afraid someone else would hear him, "sometimes I miss them... very much." And he laid his head in my lap and started crying.

15

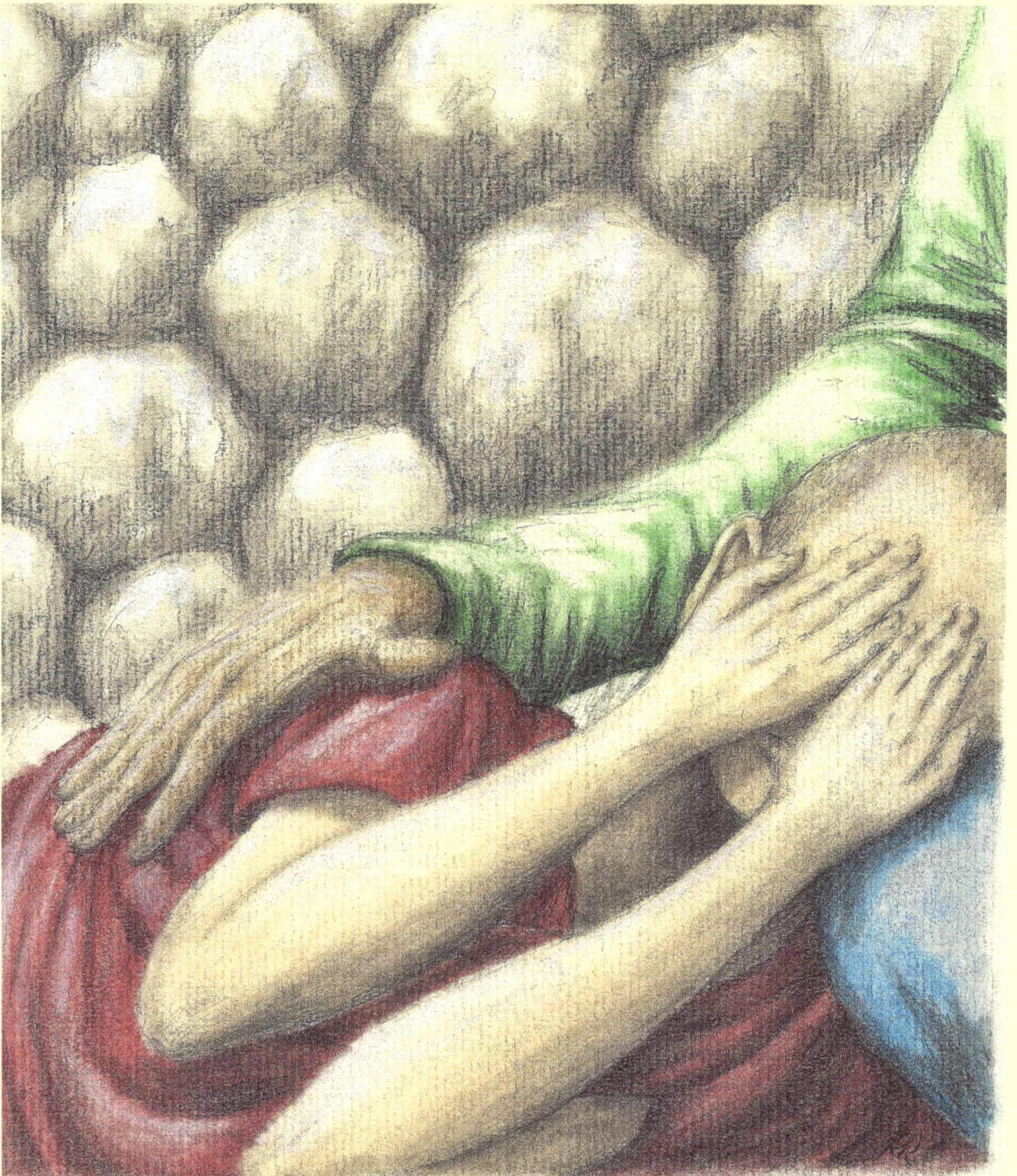

I stroked his back softly and waited patiently. When he was finished, I asked him to tell me about them.

"I am a star," he told me smiling with eyes
that twinkled just like real stars do.

17

"When I lived in the sky, we ran and ran, and ran," he laughed.

"When I lived in the sky, there were so many wonderful things. "

"We watched clouds of many colours. Some were gold and azure and pink."

"We listened to the sound of light unfurl
and stretch its fingers out to sing with us."

"We laughed in joy when the New Ones were born and taught them how to travel."

"We sang to the Old Ones as their lights grew dim, so they would not be lonely or afraid."

20

"We danced with all the worlds as they spun 'round and 'round, and 'round forever," he cried, leaping to his feet to twirl and twist and swirl and dance.

"But my favourite thing to do," he told me
giggling, "was to visit the many people on the
many planets."

"There are so many planets," he told me,
face bright and alive now, "and on them there
are so many types of people!"

I smiled, for I thought he was pretending. "Tell me about them," I asked.

His smile deepened and he closed his eyes and stretched his hands out wide into the air to explain.

"Some are very bright," he said, "brighter
than the sun! Your eyes won't hurt if you look
at them though, for they are very kind."

24

"Some live in the water. They swim with
tails that shimmer like jewels!"

"Some look like trees, with hair like
leaves of green and gold and red."

"And others fly like birds," he said
imagining himself among them, "diving
quickly and fearlessly!"

"Some do not use words like you or I, but sing through the voices of their hearts."

Then he opened his eyes and gave me a peculiar look. "Others, look just like you," he said softly, then he looked at his hands and laughed. "Just like me!" he shouted happily, rocking back and forth.

Time passed slowly at the monastery, with one day much like all the others. In the morning we said prayers.

Then we ate breakfast.

After breakfast, there were classes.

Then we had lunch.

The monks were very playful.
And sometimes they were loud.

They laughed together, and cried together.
We took care of one another.

During nap time, I sat on the roof
and watched the clouds.

36

Sometimes, I would spy Sonam alone,
always looking towards the sky.

One day, I received a letter
from my Grandparents.

I spoke to my dear friends, and told
them I must leave for a time.

"Do not go," Sonam said to me
softly. "I will go home soon, and I want
to take you with me."

I knew I would probably never see him again, so I stooped and gave him a hug. "Sonam, I must visit my Grandparents, for they are worried. They live far from here, and I must travel many days to reach them. Perhaps, I can come with you when I return," I told him gently.

41

Sonam did not smile when I looked at him again. There were no tears, but it looked like he would cry. "Do not go," he said again, voice smaller than the tiniest bird singing in the night.

"Sonam, I love you," I said. And with
that, we said goodbye.

The journey to Kathmandu was long.

Sometimes, the roads were blocked
with stones. Other times, the roads were
blocked with people.

In Kathmandu, there were many
special places, but none were
as special as my monastery.

46

The wait in the airport was long; the flight, even longer. But on the plane, outside the window, I saw something very special.

Everyone was asleep, and I looked
outside to watch the sunset.
Suddenly there was a rainbow,
and a beautiful, bright, star.

*I will go home soon, and
I want to take you with me.*

I remembered Sonam's words and
felt the tears begin to fall.

It's been many years now since I lived in Nepal, and sometimes, I go there in my dreams.

I remember the white-throated crows, and the way the ravens sang. I remember the way the dogs barked, and the little white dog who protected the monastery.

I remember the way the people came to do *kora*; the way they danced, and the way they laughed and prayed. I remember the sight of a perfect moon, mirrored perfectly on the roof, gleaming brilliantly through a puddle in the night.

I remember many things. But most of all,
I remember my friend Sonam, the Star.

Brian Gueyser (on the right in photo) is an author hailing from the Great Lakes. He enjoys sharing great meals with close friends, amazingly delicious cuisine, and the quiet embrace of Nature's gentle solitude. His favourite colour is green. As his first published work, *Sonam The Star* marks his formal entry into authorhood.

Rick Wenning II is an artist of 47 years, living in the small town of Eaton, Ohio, where he grew up. He started drawing comics out of the newspaper at age 4 and never stopped. At 16 he picked up painting and grew into a world surrounded by art. He has discovered many different mediums along the way to express his artistic needs, and there isn't a day that goes by that he doesn't think of something in a creative art form. Illustration in all its forms is truly a passion for Rick. Being a family man now with a wife and children, has given him inspiration to create on a new level. This first book has brought him to a new level of art appreciation and gratitude for the talent God has given him. He hopes to encounter many more in years to come. Thank you.

www.ingramcontent.com/pod-product-compliance
Lightning Source LLC
Chambersburg PA
CBHW042001100426

42813CB00019B/2946